SENTENCED TO
LIFE

SENTENCED TO LIFE

Malcom Muggeridge
& Alan Thornhill

*A PARABLE
IN THREE
ACTS*

Thomas Nelson Publishers
Nashville • Camden • New York

Published in Nashville, Tennessee, by Thomas Nelson, Inc. and distributed in Canada by Lawson Falle, Ltd., Cambridge, Ontario.

Printed in the United States of America.

Library of Congress Cataloging in Publication Data

Muggeridge, Malcolm, 1903–
    Sentenced to life.

    I. Thornhill, Alan Edward Carlos.   II. Title.
PR6025.U5S4   1983   822'.912   83-2298
ISBN 0-8407-5839-1

SENTENCED TO LIFE was first performed at the
Westminster Theatre, London, opening on May 17, 1978,
with the following cast:

Fergus Snow	Denys Hawthorne
Eileen Vickory	Ruth Goring
Gerald Vickory	John Byron
Anna Wolfer	Susan Colverd
Dr. Derek Winter	Robin Wentworth
Lady Bassett	Mary Wimbush

Directed by
David William

Presented by Aldersgate Productions

INTRODUCTION

It was some three years before *Sentenced to Life* opened at the Westminster Theatre on May 17, 1978, that Alan Thornhill and I decided to collaborate in writing a play about euthanasia. The suggestion came from me—the result of a journalistic hunch that euthanasia was bound shortly to become a very much alive issue. After some deliberation, Thornhill fell in enthusiastically with my proposal, and we got to work, both of us convinced that legalized euthanasia, following on legalized abortion, would mean a further plunge down the slippery slope leading to a totally humanistic, amoral way of life.

Abortion and euthanasia were being sold to the public by the media in terms of compassion; the one as sparing mothers the burden of bearing unwanted children, and the other as delivering the sick and the aged from having to go on living. Obviously, we could not effectively refute such false compassion just by making our play a series of arguments, as Bernard Shaw might have done. So, from the beginning we set our faces against polemics as such and looked for a story, or rather a parable, whose unfolding would make audiences see what truly is at stake between the advocates of what they call "mercy killing" or "death with dignity" with a view to sustaining "quality of life," and those who take their stand on the sanctity of life, which precludes, equally, the murder of unborn children, the incurably sick, and the senile old.

We had a plot ready to hand in the story of a man—we made him an Oxford don, Thornhill having been one and so knowing the species well—whose wife, a concert pianist, was stricken to the point that she was totally incapacitated and dependent on help in eating and performing all her bodily functions. Enraged by her plight, and feeling herself to be useless and a burden upon others, she desperately wants to die, but is too crippled even to kill herself. So she sets about persuading and bullying her husband to do the job for her, aided in this by their joint appearance in a television programme in which she makes a passionate plea to be helped to die, and he comes out as, in principle, a supporter of mercy killing. When, however, it is a matter of actually getting hold of some poison and feeding it to her, he tries desperately to excuse himself, but at last succumbs to her bullying and cajoling and does what she wants. She dies typing a message with her toes to the effect that it is she who has persuaded her husband to do what he has done, against his own wishes and purpose, hoping thereby to save him from the consequences of his deed.

So far so good. Up to this point the play was acceptable; our characters had expressed their different attitudes without any particular preference being shown for any one of them. It was the last act, with its Christian implications, that was out of step with the prevailing consensus, and so liable to give offence.

Gerald Vickory returns home after his time in prison and trial for murder, a different person, holding different views, and looking at life, his own and the world's around him, in a quite different way. Though he only gets a suspended sentence, he is conscious of being a convicted murderer and of his desperate need for repentance and regeneration. The arguments for euthanasia that he once expounded so glibly, now seem shallow and unconvincing; he sees his crime as particularly odious in that it was not passion that led him into it, nor even any egotis-

tical purpose, but just a vague acceptance of a principle
—mercy killing—as being compassionate, enlightened,
progressive. Now, he sees what he has done in the light
of the stark realities of Good and Evil, and realises that
he has, as it were, absentmindedly chosen the latter.

In consensus terms, this will not do; the categories of
Good and Evil are nowadays not to be taken as the ultimate criteria in any moral assessment of human conduct.
Ethics are situational, not absolute, and what human beings do, even to the point of assisting one another to die,
is a factor, not of whether the act itself is good or bad but
of the persons concerned and of the circumstances in
which it was committed. Hence it follows that euthanasia, provided it is in response to a genuinely felt wish,
is no more murder than is the destruction of a fetus in
process of developing into a fully formed, but for one
reason or another unwanted, child in its mother's womb.

From Thornhill's and my point of view, of course,
Gerald Vickory's repentance, and subsequent moral and
spiritual regeneration, is essentially what our play is
about; leave that out, and it is mere "theatre," which, in
itself, is of no great interest to either of us. Our essential
purpose was, first, to present the contemporary dilemma
of a husband under pressure from a hopelessly handi-
capped wife to provide her with the means to kill herself;
then, to show how, having yielded to this pressure, the
consequent suffering, humiliation, and remorse lead him
to break out of his cocoon of fantasy into the reality of
God's creation and of the Incarnation which alone eluci-
dates it. Solzhenitsyn in his *Gulag Archipelago* trilogy
describes how, in the same sort of way, illumination
came to him while, as he puts it, "lying on rotting prison

straw," enabling him to realise as never before what the apostle Paul calls the glorious liberty of the children of God, when, in human terms, he had no liberty at all. It might seem a far cry from this heroic soul to our Oxford don. Yet, essentially the same process has taken place in him as in Solzhenitsyn; out of suffering came the same prospect of salvation, accompanied by the same joy. For him, too, in the darkness a great light shines; after the Crucifixion comes the Resurrection, and the Cross stands, a symbol of everlasting hope, equally in the wreckage of a shallow, sheltered life as in the desolation of a prison camp. Looming behind the working of Vickory's distracted mind is the realisation that the most unmerciful killing—crucifixion—and the least dignified death—on a cross—gave rise to a tidal wave of love and creativity that has provided the Western world with its religion, its *mores*, its art and literature, its music and its cathedrals, for two thousand years.

It was not sufficient for us to convey all this just verbally; we needed an additional character in the play who would express in terms of a simple faith and purity what Gerald Vickory was going to have to confront following his surrender to his wife's determination to die and of all that resulted therefrom. Thornhill and I were well aware of the hazards of such a device; how easily it might lead to bathos and and sentimentality. Nonetheless, we decided to risk it, and introduced into our cast the *au pair* girl, Anna, to fill this role. Thanks to the patience and perceptiveness of the play's director and producer, David William, in choosing, out of some thirty auditions, Susan Colverd for the part, we had an actress who not only managed to portray Anna just as we had envisaged her, but somehow *was* her. All concerned, even hostile critics, were unanimous in praising the sincerity and convincingness of Susan's performance. I shall always treasure the memory of it, and of her, as, I am sure, will Thornhill, too.

The collaboration between Thornhill and myself in writing the play was so close that it would be difficult now, if not impossible, to disentangle which parts he or I wrote. Thornhill was more at home with dons and their ways and diction, I with television procedures and practitioners. How many Ferguses I have known and worked with! The play opens on camera with the word: "Action!" and closes on camera with the word: "Cut!" In between, the cameras occasionally show a little red light, indicating that they have come into action; otherwise they are quiescent. Their presence on the stage throughout the play signifies fantasy, active and passive.

My hunch that euthanasia was going to be a lively issue proved to be correct. At the same time as our play was running at the Westminster Theatre, another—Brian Clark's *Whose Life Is It Anyway?*—based on a very similar theme but reaching the opposite conclusion to ours, was playing to packed houses at the Mermaid Theatre. Tom Conti took the leading part; his performance was universally, and I am sure deservedly, praised. The play's assumption throughout, without any serious consideration of a contrary view, that euthanasia was justified in terms of expediency and was ethically acceptable, likewise met with general approval. The *Daily Mail* drama critic spoke for the consensus when he wrote: "Tom Conti's eloquent pleas to be allowed to embrace death with dignity at the Mermaid Theatre nightly moves its audience to an ecstasy of enthusiasm." On the other hand, he goes on: "Efforts over at the Westminster Theatre to convince us that life is a sacred flame which must burn to the bitter end, succeed only in making the exit signs like stars pointing the way to heaven." The BBC, too, after some laudatory remarks about *Whose Life Is It Anyway?*, dismissed *Sentenced to Life* as treating the same subject "in a superficial manner."

Then, when *Sentenced to Life* was in rehearsal, Derek Humphry, a journalist on the London *Sunday Times* and later on the Los Angeles *Times*, announced in a book, *Jean's Way*, that in response to his wife's strong request to have her life ended—she was suffering from cancer which had reached an advanced stage and was considered to be medically incurable—he had given her a fatal dose of poison. Despite Humphry's avowal of having committed what was still technically a crime, the Director of Public Prosecutions decided that no legal proceedings should be instituted, thereby preparing the way for legalizing euthanasia, or at any rate turning a blind eye on its practice, just as the acquittal of Dr. Aleck Bourne in 1938, after he had performed an abortion on a girl of fourteen who had been raped by several guardsmen, prepared the way for legalizing abortion. Subsequently, Dr. Bourne was so appalled by the ever-increasing number of abortions, being performed at all ages following his acquittal, that he reversed his attitude and became an ardent supporter of the pro-life movement. There are no present signs that Humphry is moving in this direction.

Both *Sentenced to Life* and *Jean's Way* deal with the same situation—of a man who is persuaded to take upon himself the responsibility of providing a desperately sick wife with the means to destroy herself. Their own reaction to what they have done is, however, quite different. Humphry considers, and presumably goes on considering, that helping his wife to die was a true act of mercy, whereas Vickory, after giving his wife poison to drink and being convicted in a law-court of murdering her, is burdened with an overwhelming sense of guilt, from which, as he comes to see, the only escape lies in the forgiveness offered to all followers of Christ who truly repent and unfeignedly believe His gospel of love.

In a dialogue with Humphry on BBC Television, the gap, or rather chasm, between us remained unbridged, even though I readily admitted that, as a professed atheist, he was perfectly entitled to fall in with his late wife's wish to die and provide her with the means to end her life. If there was no God, nor any transcendental purpose in the experience of living in this world, then a human being's life was no more intrinsically sacred than is that of a broiler-house chicken, which, if it stops laying eggs, or is otherwise incapacitated, no longer rates its allowance of chicken feed and has its neck wrung. As just part of the world's livestock, human beings may legitimately be treated similarly—as, indeed, they are in the numerous avowedly atheistic countries of our time, and as they will be in others as and when they deliberately follow suit or simply drift into taking a similar position. If we are veritably no more than livestock, then a developing fetus is indeed just so much jelly, to be thrown away with other hospital waste if the child it will become happens for one reason or another to be unwanted. Likewise, any considered to be fatally ill, mentally defective, epileptic, senile, or whoever may be regarded as missing out on the "quality of life," being incapacitated for one reason or another from having a "meaningful" existence, are euthanasia-fodder, to be disposed of by whatever means—hypodermic, withdrawal of support mechanisms, over-sedation—are conveniently available.

In Christian terms, of course, such an attitude is quite indefensible. Jesus healed the sick, raised Lazarus from the dead, gave back sanity to the deranged, but never did He practice, or include, killing as part of the mercy that occupied His heart. His true followers cannot but adopt the same attitude. For instance, Mother Teresa, of Calcutta goes to great trouble to have brought into her Home for the Dying, derelicts from the streets who may survive for no more than a quarter of an hour, but in that quarter of an hour, instead of being abandoned, they find themselves in the presence of Christian love and care. From a purely humanitarian or welfare point of view, the effort involved in this ministry of love could be put to more useful purposes and the derelicts left to die in the streets, or even helped to die by giving them an appropriate injection. Such calculations do not come into Mother Teresa's way of looking at things; her love and compassion reach out to the afflicted without any other consideration than their immediate need. She gives all she has at once, and then finds she has more to give. In the television programme, *Something Beautiful for God*, there is a shot of her holding a minute baby girl who has been found in a dustbin and is so minute that you wonder that she can exist at all. As commentator, I ask Mother Teresa whether, in view of India's alleged over-population and general penury, it is really worthwhile salvaging this little creature, to which she replies by lifting her up and saying exultantly: "See, there's life in her!" For me, the picture and the words provide a perfect answer to those who claim that by killing babies before they come into the world, and expediting the departure of the decrepit, the sick, and the old from the world, the quality of life can be enhanced.

In my dialogue with Derek Humphry I referred to an incident in my own life, which, though it happened long ago, stands out in my mind as a sort of parable about this whole issue of euthanasia—a study, as it were, in mercy living in contradistinction to mercy killing. Some forty years ago, shortly before the outbreak of the 1939–45 war, the person whom I have most loved in this world, my wife, Kitty, was desperately ill, and, as I was informed, had only an outside chance of surviving. The medical details are unimportant; probably today, with the great advances that have taken place in curative medicine, her state would not be so serious. But as the situation presented itself then, she was hovering between life and death, though, needless to say, there was no voice, as there might be in comparable circumstances nowadays, to suggest that it would perhaps be better to let her go.

The doctor explained that an emergency operation was essential, and in honesty, he had to tell me that it would be something of a gamble. Her blood, it seemed, was so thin that before he operated a blood-transfusion was desperately needed—this was before the days of plasma. As he said this, a feeling of happiness amounting to ecstasy surged up inside me. If I could be the donor! My blood was found to be suitable for the transfusion; the necessary gear was brought in, very primitive by contemporary standards—just a glass tube, one end of which was inserted in her arm and the other end in mine, with a pump in the middle drawing out my blood and sending it into her. I could watch the flow, shouting out absurdly to the doctor: "Don't stint yourself; take all you want!" and noting with delight the immediate effect in bringing back life into her face that before had seemed grey and lifeless. It was the turning-point; from that moment she began to mend.

At no point in our long relationship was there a more ecstatic moment than when I thus saw my life-blood pouring into hers to revivify her. We were at one, blood to blood, as no other kind of union could make us. To give life—this was what love was for; to give it in all circumstances and eventualities, whereas to take it away, whether from a fertilized ovum even one second after conception, or from some drooling imbecile or senile octogenarian or anguished sufferer from a fatal sickness, was the denial of life and the antithesis of love. Seen in life-denying terms, compassion easily becomes a holocaust—witness the millions of unborn babies now being destroyed each year in compassionate abortions. Dostoevsky made the same point when he wrote: "Love toward men, but love without belief in God, very naturally leads to the greatest coercion over men, and turns their lives completely into hell on earth."

The translation of a compassionate purpose that is godless and without love, into a realisation of death and diabolism on a gigantic scale, is made manifest in the holocaust that befell Hitler's Germany. This holocaust has lately been shown to television viewers in many countries to the accompaniment of much appropriate breast-beating, but an essential consideration has been left out—that the origins of the holocaust lay not in Nazi terrorism and anti-Semitism but in pre-Nazi Weimar Germany's acceptance of mercy-killing as a humane practice. Even while the penitential holocaust was being shown on American, and then on German and other Western European TV screens, yet another holocaust was getting under way, this time in the countries that had defeated Hitler's Third Reich, and, at the Nuremburg Tribunal, condemned as a war crime the propositions and practices on which the Nazi holocaust was based. No one could have put the matter more cogently and explicitly than has Dr. Leo Alexander, now a Boston psychiatrist, who in 1946–47 was consultant to the U.S. Secretary of War, and on duty with the office of chief counsel for war crimes at Nuremburg.

Reporting on war crimes relating to the holocaust, Dr. Alexander writes:

Whatever proportion of these crimes finally assumed, it became evident to all who investigated them that they had started from small beginnings. The beginnings at first were merely a subtle shift in emphasis in the basic attitudes of the physicians. It started with the acceptance of the attitude, basic in the euthanasia movement, that there is such a thing as life not worthy to be lived. This attitude in its early stages concerned itself merely with the severely and chronically sick. Gradually, the sphere of those to be included in this category was enlarged to encompass the socially unproductive, the ideologically unwanted, the racially unwanted, and finally all non-Germans. *But it is im-*

portant to realise that the infinitely small wedged-in lever from which the entire trend of mind received its impetus was the attitude towards the nonrehabilitable sick (my italics).

In the final analysis, then, the issue on which *Sentenced to Life* is based, and which it seeks to elucidate, is simply whether our human society is to be seen as a factory-farm, or, as it has been seen through the Christian centuries, as a family whose father is a loving God. If the latter, then from the moment of conception a fetus is potentially a human soul, with all that implies, and a mongoloid child or old derelict no less precious in the Creator's eyes than a beauty queen or a Mensa IQ.

Either we in the West go on with the process of shaping our own destiny without reference to any higher being than man, deciding ourselves how many children should be born, when, and in what varieties, and which lives should be continued and which cut short; or we draw back, seeking to understand and fall in with our Creator's purposes for us rather than to pursue our own, in true humility praying, as the founder of our religion and our civilisation taught us: *Thy will be done.*

I should not wish to suggest that these moral simplicities can be readily translated into a clear course of action in our contemporary day-to-day living; when men and women tangle with them, the result is often confusion and great suffering.

It is to explore this aspect that Alan Thornhill and I have written our play *Sentenced to Life,* which turns on a stricken woman's desire to die and a husband's reluctant falling in with her wishes.

The play offers no rule-of-thumb judgments, but it does, as we hope, bring out the spiritual considerations in a dilemma that today is too often seen purely in terms of economics and personal comfort.

MALCOLM MUGGERIDGE
December 1982

CHARACTERS
IN ORDER OF APPEARANCE:

		AGE
FERGUS SNOW	TV director/producer	40
EILEEN VICKORY	Former concert pianist; now an invalid	40
GERALD VICKORY	Her husband, and English literature don at Oxford	45
ANNA WOLFER	Their German *au pair*	22
DR. DEREK WINTER	Eileen's physician	50
LADY BASSETT	Honorary Secretary of the Right to Die Movement	60

SUNDRY TV
TECHNICAL STAFF

Except for the Prologue, the action takes place in the living room of the Vickorys' house in Oxford, England.

Time:	The 1970s
PROLOGUE:	A television interview in a studio
ACT I:	An evening in autumn
ACT II:	Morning—a week later
ACT III:	Afternoon—four months later

23

PROLOGUE

Television studio. Furniture covered in blacks. Technicians scuttle, tidying studio. Lighting technician comes in, does lighting check through lanterns.

Floor manager enters. Checks studio ready. Interview chairs in place.

On cue Eileen, still a beautiful woman, is pushed in wheelchair by her husband Gerald, somewhat older. Enter Fergus, smooth and calculating. Meets Gerald and Eileen. Wheelchair is placed on markers by floor manager. Make-up girl attends to participants. Another girl holds portable clock.

Television cameramen take their places. Floor manager starts countdown. Until now action has been in silence.

FLOOR MANAGER: Stand-by Studio—recording in one minute.
Start the clock, please.
(Pause)

Forty seconds.
Thirty seconds.
O.K., Fergus.

FERGUS: Right. Interview with Gerald and Eileen Vickory to be used as part of *Way of Life* programme on mercy killing. *Way of Life.* 2279 stroke 3.

27

FLOOR
MANAGER: Ten seconds—good luck everyone.
            Five, four, three . . . ACTION!
            (Cues Fergus with arm cue)

FERGUS: With me tonight are Gerald Vickory, Lec-
            turer in English Literature at Oxford
            University, author of several books in-
            cluding the recent critical biography of
            George Meredith—Mr. Vickory is also
            Honorary Treasurer of the United Free-
            doms League—and his wife, Eileen.
            Apart from slight movement in her toes,
            head, and neck, Mrs. Vickory is totally
            paralysed. Before she was incapacitated,
            she was familiar to the musical public as
            Eileen Mansfield, the distinguished con-
            cert pianist. Mrs. Vickory, when did it
            first hit you—this tragic illness—and
            what exactly is it?

EILEEN: They tell me it's a form of acute infective
            polyneuritis. About precisely what form,
            the experts seem unable to make up their
            minds. It happened about two years ago.
            "Hit me" is right. It's like a thunderbolt.
            One day you're your normal, active self,
            and then suddenly, out of the blue, that
            hideous, volcanic pain in the head and
            neck—every movement a torture. Then a
            congealing, a seizing up of every limb,
            every muscle, till it becomes a struggle to
            stand, to raise an arm, to turn over. A lit-
            tle later you find you can't swallow, you
            can't even blink, every breath is an ago-

nising wrench that you feel must be the last. When Gerald took me to the hospital, I was barely able to walk to the car. By the time we got there, I couldn't move.

FERGUS: What did it feel like?

EILEEN: Sometimes you knew where you were. Sometimes you were in a swirling river, being dragged down. You don't really think. You just fight. For the next breath, the next minute. Something keeps you going.

GERALD: She won't tell you how brave she was, how valiantly she fought every inch of the way back to life. That's what the doctors said—she did it herself. Otherwise she'd have gone under.

EILEEN: That's when I still thought there was a hope of recovery. Oh yes, you're manoeuvred, manipulated, taught how to eat and to speak, to breathe all over again. Everyone is wonderful. Everyone congratulates you, and the doctors congratulate themselves on having pulled you through. You're fitted up with all sorts of ingenious devices for managing with only a fraction of your body operative. You can learn to do all sorts of things with your toes—turn on the light, dial the telephone, even use a special typewriter. But they haven't developed a keyboard yet for me to play Beethoven with my toes. Maybe that will come.

FERGUS: How do you feel about it now?

EILEEN: Angry. Furiously angry with myself, with everyone, with life, even with the God I don't believe in. No, I wish I had gone under. It would have been more merciful, more humane.

FERGUS: Gerald, you're a well-known upholder of human rights, and of course you're personally involved in this tragic case. What do you feel about euthanasia?

GERALD: *(Donnish)* Euthanasia, as I'm sure you know, Fergus, is derived from two Greek words: *thanatos*, meaning death, and the prefix *eu*, meaning easy or good. Certainly no one could disapprove of an easy or good death.

FERGUS: Yes, but in practice . . .

GERALD: I have for many years now, as you were kind enough to suggest, Fergus, been a strong advocate of individual liberty, of the right of each person to control, as far as possible, his own destiny. That surely must include the right to die, with dignity.

FERGUS: What exactly do you mean by that?

GERALD: I think there are situations when death should not be the master summoning us in his own time and manner, but the servant whom we summon to do our bidding. You probably know the line, "I have a rendezvous with death." Should we not sometimes have the right to choose the time and place of that rendezvous?

FERGUS: Would you agree with that, Mrs. Vickory?

EILEEN: I certainly would. You'll find plenty of people to say that they've been purified by affliction, that looking after the afflicted is a great enrichment of life, that a loving God puts suffering in the world to enhance the experience of living, all part of the great drama He mounts, involving us all. Well, I don't believe any of it. The third of me that's alive and articulate demands the right to join the other two-thirds that's dead. Only you see, I can't bring it about myself. I can't lift a cup to my lips, I can't find a vein and cut it. I can't even fall out of this chair or sink under water in the bath. *(With rising fury)* I'm imprisoned in life, and I'm battering on the walls, crying, "Help! I want to get out! Help! Help!"

GERALD: *(Getting up in great agitation and going to her)* She doesn't mean it. Why should she have fought to live if she had just wanted to die?

FERGUS: O.K. Hold it there.

FLOOR MANAGER: Cut!

FERGUS: *(To Eileen)* That was marvellous. *(Ad lib)* Just what we wanted. O.K., everybody.

(Exit in blackout)

ACT I

*Piano music in background. In the black-
out the television studio is transformed
into the Vickory living room. Eileen on a
couch and Gerald are watching the trans-
mission of the television programme.
Anna (young German au pair) watches
too, lying on the floor. The cameras re-
main on stage throughout the play, mute
and symbolic.*

EILEEN'S
VOICE ON
TV:
Only you see, I can't bring it about myself. I can't lift a cup to my lips, I can't
find a vein and cut it. I can't even fall out
of this chair or sink under water in the
bath. I'm imprisoned in life, and I'm battering on the walls, crying, "Help! I want
to get out! Help! Help!"

*(Gerald moves quickly over to TV and
turns it off)*

EILEEN: Why did you turn it off before the end?

GERALD: That was the end for all intents and purposes. Your last speech, so beautifully
done, so dramatic.

EILEEN: Your last speech was dramatic, too.

GERALD: I didn't want to hear it.

EILEEN: Why not?

GERALD: It was embarrassingly emotional.

EILEEN: Fergus liked it all right.

GERALD: He would. Those TV people love to catch you off guard.

EILEEN: Speaking the truth, you mean. For once.

GERALD: The point is you were so convincing. I almost took it literally.

EILEEN: How do you think I looked? *(Gerald gives her wine from a glass)*

GERALD: Stunning. *(Vaguely)* That lovely . . .

EILEEN: It was a caftan.

GERALD: Well. You looked beautiful, as ever. What do you think, Anna? What's the matter with you?

ANNA: *(Very upset)* Please excuse, *Herr* Professor. Perhaps I did not understand. *(With difficulty)* But never should they be allowed to do it.

EILEEN: Not "Never should they be allowed," Anna. Say, "They should never be allowed to do it." Yours is a German construction.

ANNA: In our German schools they have always taught us how the Nazis has killed the old and helpless. Is it not this that you British people has fought against? Now will you do it for yourselves?

GERALD: Of course not. We were not talking about gas-chambers, Anna. That was the work of madmen, of monsters.

ANNA: But before the madmen, the monsters, there was a law; oh yes, very scientific, like you, so *akademisch*, meaning so well. Doctors, professors were consenting. "We build up a strong, healthy, clear race. So the rest we throw away."

GERALD: That has nothing to do with the right to die.

ANNA: The right to die, will be, one day, I think, the right to kill. At the end, is not so far separated.

GERALD: That could be a point for discussion. You must understand, Anna, that in our country we have open civilised debate on controversial topics, and we give free scope for every point of view.

ANNA: Oh, excuse me. So you talk only. *(To Eileen)* So you have not meant what you have said about wanting to be killed?

EILEEN: *(Correcting her)* "You did not mean what you said."

ANNA: *(Turning to Gerald)* She did not mean what she said.

GERALD: Yes and no.

ANNA: I do not understand. Please excuse. I go and play Beethoven. He means what he has said. *(Exit)*

EILEEN: Well, don't let him say it too loudly—and get the phrasing right.

GERALD: A regular little *Fräulein Götterdammerung* tonight, isn't she? Shall I tell her to lay off the music?

EILEEN: Don't bother. She needs it. Lets off steam.

GERALD: She's somewhat hysterical; like all Germans. They're all so horribly literal. Everything's black and white, either or, *entweder oder*.

EILEEN: There is something a bit *entweder oder* about death, you have to admit. She does get on one's nerves. We probably should never have brought her over. *(Playing starts off—the* Pathétique *Sonata)* Her playing isn't all that good. I thought there

38

was something special about it when we first heard her on that terrible farm piano. I wanted to give her a chance.

GERALD: You've helped her tremendously. Taught her so much.

EILEEN: Probably I'm envious that she should be able to play, and I, so incomparably better, can't.

GERALD: We can always send her back. Find someone else.

EILEEN: That's all very well, Gerald. She feeds me, washes me, gets me to bed, gets me up. She knows how. You don't know how ghastly it is dealing with someone who doesn't. You, for instance. That's the trouble. I'm dependent on her, and yet she upsets me. She's so physical somehow. Besides, she's mad on you, and that's vaguely irritating.

GERALD: Don't be ridiculous, Eileen.

EILEEN: She has a picture of you by her bed. Not one of both of us. Just you. And I bet she kisses it goodnight.

GERALD: Well, so long as she sticks to the picture.

EILEEN: You try giving her half a chance!

GERALD: Nonsense! She's a child, and rather a stupid one at that. I'm just a father figure. She's not even pretty.

EILEEN: I know that, but she's alive all through, not like me, just in the upper part. Have you ever thought, Gerald, that though the operative part of sex is in the dead part of my body, the switch, as it were, is in the live part? The switch, but no current. Anna's all current.

GERALD: That sounds sick, Eileen dear; don't indulge it. *(Front doorbell rings)* That's the doctor. He said he was looking in this evening. *(At door)* Anna. Would you mind answering the door? I think it's Dr. Winter.

ANNA: *(Off)* Certainly, *Herr* Professor.

EILEEN: You see what I mean. "Yes, *Herr* Professor. Certainly, *Herr* Professor." I keep telling her you're not a Professor; just a plain, ordinary don.

GERALD: Oh, in Germany, if you're half-literate you're a professor.

EILEEN: Exactly! Quick, Gerald, find my lipstick. I may at least look half-human.

GERALD: There isn't time.

EILEEN: The doctor can wait.

GERALD: Doctors don't wait. *(Fumbling)* Where is it?

EILEEN: In my bag. Use your eyes. Now, Gerald, for goodness sake stop flapping. The other end, stupid.

GERALD: I never know how to do this.

EILEEN: Come on. Just think you're underlining a very important point in a book you're going to review. Mind my teeth. I don't want to swallow it.

GERALD: How's that?

EILEEN: Well, let me have the mirror and look. I'm not clairvoyant. *(Gerald finds mirror and holds it up)* I said underline; not illuminate the whole text.

GERALD: I'm sorry. Is that better? *(Cleaning off face)*

EILEEN: Smeary, but passable. Gerald, I want to have a word with the doctor. Leave us alone, will you, please?

GERALD: That suits me. *(At door)* Come in, Derek.

DR. WINTER: *(Entering)* Good evening. Sorry to be so late. It's been a busy day. All this 'flu about.

GERALD: Well, I'll leave you to it. I must go through tomorrow's lecture. I usually put in a new joke every two or three years. I'll see you before you go. *(Exit)*

DR. WINTER: Well, Mrs. Vickory, how are we getting on?

EILEEN: I don't know how *you're* getting on, doctor. As far as I'm concerned, I'm stuck, hopelessly stuck.

DR. WINTER: I do understand how you must feel at times, believe me. By the way, I told that German girl of yours to keep on playing. I hope you approve. I think she's good.

EILEEN: She's not bad. We stayed in her parents' farm when we were on that skiing holiday in Bavaria.

DR. WINTER: The pulse is fine. Quite normal. I'm sure you'll be delighted to know the specialists have finally agreed on the nature of your infection. They refer to it as . . .

EILEEN: I don't want to hear it. Call me a medical mystery. "Vickoryitis." All I want to know is, shall I recover?

DR. WINTER: "Recover," I'm afraid, is not the operative word. There should be no serious deterioration. In fact you may well have slight improvements. You have a great deal to be thankful for.

EILEEN: Have I?

DR. WINTER: *(As he talks he is trying various movements of her arms and fingers)* Well, you're alive. Believe me, there were many days and weeks when that seemed extremely unlikely. You've progressed from an iron lung to a respirator to being able now to breathe quite on your own. How is the breathing, by the way? Let me hear you. Breathe. Breathe. Again. *(Using his stethoscope)*

EILEEN: You do realise that I have to think to breathe? If I stop thinking, I stop breathing.

DR. WINTER: You will learn to manage these things better and better. I think there's a little movement in that middle finger. Try it again. Concentrate. Think harder! Again!

43

Good! There is a sign of distinct advance. At least here you are, back in your own home.

EILEEN: Well, I admit it's better than looking out at those dirty grey rooftops.

DR. WINTER: It's a beautiful room, Mrs. Vickory, and your husband has arranged everything superbly. All the latest equipment. I understand you are able to turn on the television by manipulating your toes. *(Examining feet)*

EILEEN: Turning on TV with your toes is hardly the full life.

DR. WINTER: Then you can enjoy the music.

EILEEN: Yes, but do you suppose it's easy to lie here and listen to my pieces being played on my piano by my pupil? Oh, I know that sounds very mean and petty. But when you are completely dependent on someone to feed you, wash you, lift you, blow your nose, and etcetera you, I find it tends to meanness and pettiness. Talking of blowing noses, would you please ask that girl to stop playing and come and blow my nose. It's tickling.

DR. WINTER: Don't disturb her. Let me.

44

EILEEN: It's her job to be disturbed. Besides, relief from the piano will be a boon.

DR. WINTER: If you insist.

EILEEN: No—just a moment, while we're alone. I'm so seldom alone. Doctor, I want to ask you to do something for me.

DR. WINTER: *(Wipes her nose)* I'll do anything I can within reason.

EILEEN: This is wholly within reason, and quite easy.

DR. WINTER: Well?

EILEEN: I want you to end my life.

DR. WINTER: I don't follow exactly.

EILEEN: It's perfectly simple, isn't it? You must know dozens of ways of doing it. Choose a nice painless one.

DR. WINTER: I don't think you know what you are saying.

EILEEN: Did you see us on TV tonight?

DR. WINTER: I'm afraid I seldom watch the TV.

EILEEN: Look, Doctor, I've thought it out with the

utmost care and objectivity. Surely you believe in freedom for the individual—like Gerald.

DR. WINTER: Yes.

EILEEN: Doesn't that include the right to die? I'd do it myself any day. The irony is that in my particular state, I not only can't live in any true sense of the word, I can't even die without help. I want your help, that's all.

DR. WINTER: Quite. I think you'd better relax for a moment. *(Pops thermometer into her mouth).* I will do my utmost to help you to live. I certainly will not help you to die. It would be committing a crime.

EILEEN: *(Spitting out thermometer)* Isn't this a crime? Letting me...go on in what is nothing more than...*(Doctor puts thermometer in again)*

DR. WINTER: Mrs. Vickory, I'm a doctor. My task, as I see it, is to try to make life for you, and all my patients, as full, as bearable, as healthy as I possibly can. Beyond that I cannot go. I have a great deal of sympathy with your theories about the right to die, and of course with you personally. But believe me, whatever the theory, whatever legislation may be brought in in the future, someone in the end will be called up to do the fatal deed. And that will probably be a doctor like me. But until then, I abide by the rules. *(Reading temperature)* Normal!

EILEEN: Well, I'm glad something's normal. Come on, Doctor, get it over with quietly and decently. You doctors do it all the time; you know you do.

DR. WINTER: We never, what you call "do it," in cases such as yours. Believe me.

EILEEN: Oh, I know you are all wonderful. You've saved my life. You've even identified my disease. But this is not life. *(Trying to shout)* Oh Anna! For God's sake, shut up.

DR. WINTER: You mustn't shout or get excited. Every breath is precious.

ANNA: *(Entering)* Have you called, Eileen?

EILEEN: That *Pathétique* Sonata is getting horribly *pathétique*. That first movement is marked *Gravé*, not gravy. And there are all sorts of naughty little rubatos popping up all over the place. It tends to sentimentality. *Schwarmerei.*

47

ANNA: I'm sorry. I try to remember the way you played it.

EILEEN: You should have heard Schnäbel play it. We'll talk about it later. But lay off for a bit now. Oh, and while you're here, blow my nose, will you?

ANNA: *Natürlich.*

EILEEN: And now, hop it. I don't want to be disturbed. I'll call you when I'm ready for bed.

ANNA: How you tell it. *(Exit)*

DR. WINTER: I don't think you're quite fair.

EILEEN: I know. But I shall get worse and worse unless you or someone helps me.

DR. WINTER: What about your husband? What does he feel about all this?

EILEEN: Oh, don't worry about him. He's always been for it, long before these last two years.

DR. WINTER: He would approve of your taking your own life?

EILEEN: In theory, yes. That's where intellectuals

like him are so impossible. He'd be for it, but would he help bring it about? Abortion? Oh yes, so long as I don't have to throw the little wriggling embryo into the dustbin. Bloody revolution? By all means, so long as it's somebody else's blood. Gerald lives in poetic dramas with the stage littered with corpses. The sight of a real one would scare him to death.

DR. WINTER: How can a man kill someone he loves?

EILEEN: Look, doctor, you people have found out all about my fascinating illness. I'm of no interest any more. "Operation successful; patient dies." Isn't that the logical sequence? You can all have a lovely post mortem. You can have more. I'll make a bargain with the medical profession: do as I ask, and then you can auction me for spare parts. Then you really might be saving a life.

DR. WINTER: Mrs. Vickory, I'm afraid I cannot continue this conversation any longer. I shall do my best to forget that it ever took place. By my examination you are making real progress, steady progress. Why, you've even learned to type with your toes.

EILEEN: Oh, yes. I'll soon be able to type a whole

article with my toes. It'll be an indictment
against all the people in this world with
ideas and ideals which they never carry
out. I shall type it with my toes and call it
"Cold Feet."

(Enter Gerald)

GERALD: May I come in? How's she getting on,
Derek?

DR. WINTER: I'd say she's extremely vigorous.

GERALD: Has the physiotherapy done any good?

DR. WINTER: We'll have to be patient. Mustn't expect
too much.

EILEEN: I don't.

DR. WINTER: I'll keep in close touch. Oh, well, I must
be pushing off now. My wife hasn't set
eyes on me since breakfast. Goodbye,
Mrs. Vickory. I do hope you'll encourage
Anna to keep playing. She sounds prom-
ising. . . . Don't bother. I'll find my own
way out. Call me, if you need me. *(Exit)*

GERALD: Derek have anything to say?

EILEEN: Nothing. I'm just someone to be coaxed
and humoured. "And how are we to-

day?" When you're crippled, people think you're half-witted too.

GERALD: Where's Anna?

EILEEN: She's upstairs. I'd leave her alone for a bit. She's probably dreaming of *Herr* Professor. He's so *philosophisch*. So *grundsätzlich*.

GERALD: *(Laughing)* So *wissenschaftlich*.

EILEEN: And so delightfully inefficient in all the practical things she can do for you, and I can't. Do you think you could rise to such heights as to make us a cup of coffee?

GERALD: Of course. *(Exit to kitchen)*

EILEEN: *(Calling after him)* You know, you came over very well on that programme. Just your usual self.

GERALD: *(Off)* I didn't quite get that. What did you say?

EILEEN: You know I can't shout. All I said was that you were your usual self.

GERALD: *(Putting head in)* What's that supposed to mean?

EILEEN: All that *eu thanatos* business—a rendez-

51

vous with death. You made death sound wonderfully donnish. I don't see how anyone could fail to be convinced.

GERALD: I'll just have a look at the milk. It won't be a minute.

EILEEN: Get me a rug, dear, will you? I'm freezing.

GERALD: Here we are! Instant service. *(Rug set. Gerald returns to kitchen. Phone rings)*

EILEEN: Telephone!

GERALD: *(Returning exasperated)* That thought had occurred to me.

EILEEN: Well, I can't answer it, can I? Hadn't you better deal with the coffee first?

GERALD: As you say. *(Rushes)*

EILEEN: Oh, forget it. Answer the phone.

GERALD: Anything to oblige. *(Goes to phone)* Gerald Vickory speaking. Yes. Oh yes, Fergus, good of you to call. . . . I'm very glad to hear that, Fergus. *(Off phone)* It's Fergus.

EILEEN: That thought had occurred to me.

GERALD: I'm just telling Eileen. *(To Eileen)* They're having dozens of phone-ins. Ecstatic! The lines are jammed. *(To phone)* Yes, Fergus. Just what you were looking for. Suitably provocative. *(To Eileen)* Fergus is boiling over with excitement.

EILEEN: So is the milk, I imagine.

GERALD: Fergus. There's been a slight domestic crisis. You want to talk to her? I think we can manage that. Hold on. *(Bringing phone, he stands holding the phone for her, unaware that he has given it the wrong way round)*

EILEEN: *(Looking exasperated)* You idiot! No, Fergus, not you. . . . What sort of a proposition? . . . Isn't one enough? . . . I don't think you'd find anything interesting in the way I live. It's the most unutterably boring subject you can imagine. But if you really want to, certainly. Come and talk to me about it whenever you like. I'm always here, you know.

GERALD: *(Taking phone)* All right, Fergus. Keep us in touch. . . . Yes, we'd like to see some of the fan mail when it comes in. . . . Not at all. Always glad to strike a blow for the cause. Goodbye. *(Hangs up)* Well, it's been a marvellous success. Constance

Bassett's been on the phone already. Says it's the best thing yet for her "Right to Die" movement.

EILEEN: The coffee! *(Gerald rushes out)*

GERALD: Just coming, darling. *(Entering with coffee)* I'm afraid there's not much coffee. Most of the milk had boiled away. Here we are. *(He adjusts cup with a glass tube)* How's that? *(She can't reach it because it is the wrong way round. Gerald adjusts it)* Sorry, dear. You were evidently the hit of the show. Fergus thinks you've got that indefinable quality that makes people think and feel. You're a natural performer.

EILEEN: I'm not a performer; and this isn't coffee.

GERALD: I'd better get Anna.

EILEEN: No! I don't want Anna, and take this thing away. I want to talk to you.

GERALD: What about?

EILEEN: Fergus thinks he might be able to use me again. I'm what's known as good TV material.

GERALD: What sort of thing did he suggest?

54

EILEEN: I don't know. Something about my day-to-day life. How I manage and manoeuvre.

GERALD: Could be exciting.

EILEEN: Except that there's one thing you seem to forget.

GERALD: What's that?

EILEEN: I won't be here.

GERALD: Whatever do you mean?

EILEEN: I'll be nothing, the dear departed.

GERALD: The what?

EILEEN: Don't you understand, I'll be dead.

GERALD: Are you trying to be funny?

EILEEN: You heard me on the programme, for goodness sake. I want to die. I have a right to die. You said it yourself.

GERALD: Yes, of course. But how?

EILEEN: I can't kill myself, can I? I need help.

GERALD: What sort of help?

EILEEN: Well, this is terribly hard to say, to find the right words. There aren't any right words.

GERALD: For what?

EILEEN: Gerald, I want an orange. Will you peel it for me?

GERALD: Certainly. There's one here. I'll give it to you in pieces.

EILEEN: Mind how you go. I don't want to get drowned in juice. I'd better have a napkin. There's one in the sideboard.

It's perfectly simple, Gerald. As simple as peeling an orange. You just feed poison instead. You can put it in the orange if you like. Only don't tell me when you're going to do it. I don't want to know.

Careful, you're going to drip.

GERALD: *(Aghast)* You can't possibly ask me to do such a thing.

EILEEN: Gerald dear, I know it's a lot to ask. An awful lot. But have you really seriously thought about me? I happen to mean what I said on TV. You obviously didn't.

If I were an animal in pain, you'd what is known as "put me out of my misery."

GERALD: But you're not an animal. You're a woman, my wife.

EILEEN: I'm in far greater misery than any animal could possibly be. Look, Gerald, this isn't the first time I've tried to ask you to do this. I've even begun to ask you before.

GERALD: When?

EILEEN: Oh, you were buried in the metaphysical poets or something, and I gave up. But tonight, you've given me my cue. You said it for me, publicly, to the great viewing audience. You told it to the camera, in other words, God. We have the right to choose. You see, for me, and I should have thought for you, it's a question of principle. If you and I can arrange this and make people understand, then it'll be that much easier for thousands of others.

GERALD: But I couldn't think of it. You must talk to the doctor.

EILEEN: I have. He won't budge. Nor will Anna. She's very narrowly brought up. You heard her. When it comes to human rights, Christians are extremely unreliable. In fact, Anna mustn't know anything about this till it's all over. She might interfere.

GERALD: Look, darling, let's talk about all this in the morning. You're tired and not quite yourself.

EILEEN: You madden me. Here you have been spouting to the vast TV audience about human rights, the right to die, *eu thanatos.* "A good death," wasn't that it? I don't believe you mean a word of it.

GERALD: I LOVE YOU, Eileen!

EILEEN: I know. I believe you do—or did. And I love you—or did. And that's why you must do this thing for me. The doctors have said I'm liable to pop off. If you're clever you might not be found out.

GERALD: After that broadcast? There'd be a post mortem. They'd know instantly.

EILEEN: Then be completely open and honest. Stick to your guns. It'll be a *cause célèbre.* You'll have the world on your side.

GERALD: Don't be flippant, Eileen.

EILEEN: Gerald, dear, I know I sound flippant. That's because I don't dare yet to be anything else. This isn't a sudden crazy impulse. I've thought about it. Don't imagine I'm not afraid sometimes. Not all of me wants to die. But more of me wants to than the bits that want to live. Please, Gerald! . . . To go to sleep and not wake up again! What bliss!

GERALD: Suppose it isn't the end. Suppose you wake up in some other state of being?

EILEEN: Religious hang-over again! You're talking like Anna. No, I'll take the risk. It's death before death that worries me. And don't imagine I haven't thought about you and what a release it will be for you to be rid of this burden, this living corpse.

GERALD: I don't understand you.

EILEEN: That's because you live on ideas and you know very little about real people.

GERALD: It's a nightmare.

EILEEN: Life is a nightmare, most of the time for most people. Look at us. Sixteen years. It's not quite what we dreamed of; and now that God, in His infinite something or other, has taken away my music, then He can have the rest of me. So, Gerald?

GERALD: Do you realise what you're asking me to do, Eileen? To murder you. And we're talking about it as though it were some quite trivial decision, like whether we should go to Glyndebourne or have an evening out in the West End. After all, we're husband and wife. We can't just rule out the past. And now you just say: "Do me a favour, kill me." Well, the answer is "No!" And I'll hear no more about it. *(Shouting)* Anna!

ANNA: *(Off)* Yes, *Herr* Professor?

GERALD: Mrs. Vickory is ready for bed now.

ANNA: Coming, *Herr* Professor. *Ich komme gleich.*

EILEEN: *(Speaking very deliberately)* You'll do what I ask, Gerald. I'll make you. *(Enter Anna)* Hello, Anna. Bedtime. It's been a long day. *(Exit Gerald)*

ANNA: *Herr* Professor runs away, I think.

EILEEN: Oh, be an angel, Anna. Give me a little massage, will you? It's so soothing. You're getting so good at it.

ANNA: *Sehr gern.*

EILEEN: Dig in a bit. Those strong fingers.

ANNA: Not too much *Schwärmerei?*

EILEEN: Ouch! Too much left hand. You're not playing Liszt. Try a nice Chopin Nocturne. Don't take my remarks too seriously, Anna—any of them.

ANNA: I believe there is always something to live for.

EILEEN: Still thinking about that silly broadcast, are you?

ANNA: You talk for the devil. And *Herr* Professor with his gentle voice and clever words was, what do you say, consenting. I could not believe it.

EILEEN: Always remember, Anna, very clever people can say very stupid things.

ANNA: But you said it together.

EILEEN: I try to be a realist. There are times when I feel I can't go on much longer.

ANNA: I do my best for help.

EILEEN: Not "for help," "to help." Oh, if only I wasn't such a heavy, useless cow.

ANNA: I look after plenty cows. I like better look after you.

EILEEN: Tell me, what kind of night is it?

ANNA: It is *prima*. There is a full moon and many stars.

EILEEN: Take me to the window, will you? I want to look out.

ANNA: Now for the quick waltz. *(Raising her and manoeuvring her into wheelchair)*

EILEEN: And turn out all the lights.

ANNA: Surely. *(She does so and pushes Eileen front stage to an imaginary window)* It is out of this earth.

EILEEN: "Out of this world."

ANNA: World.

EILEEN: *(Looking out)* It certainly is. When I was a little girl, my father used to take me to the window at night. He'd point out all the different stars and constellations by name. Do you know the stars, Anna?

ANNA: I can find *Nordstern*. You see there. We call that "the Bear."

EILEEN: So do we.

ANNA: Go up, up to the end, and . . . look, there it is. It always shows the same way.

EILEEN: Your life has fixed points, hasn't it, Anna? Mine hasn't. It did once: Music. Until your God took it away.

ANNA: If you do not believe in God, why do you hate Him so much?

EILEEN: It isn't fair. If He isn't there, I'll never be any the wiser. But if He is, why the hell didn't He let me know? Sometimes I wish I were a child again, on the threshold of life, instead of near the bloody back door.

ANNA: You must learn to be happy like once you were. *(She puts her arms round Eileen gently)* There. See, I hold you in my arms like a little girl.

EILEEN: Can you imagine Gerald doing this now?

ANNA: *(Laughs) Herr* Professor?

EILEEN: Gerald was not quite so *Herr* Professor-ish when first I knew him. Do you know where we met? I was in the Cathedral all by myself practising the organ. Bach. Toccata in F major. Suddenly there was somebody standing behind me. I went on playing. Then he was sitting on the bench beside me. I could feel him drinking in the music and everything. I don't know if it was the music or me, but we talked and talked, and later he put his arms around me.

ANNA: You loved him?

EILEEN: Yes, I did. Very much. We were both over thirty. It was very romantic. But somehow it died. We both got very busy. Apparently you can't live and love just on music and poetry. No, love ends for him in the Oxford Book of English Verse. In many ways he's more deprived than I am. Keep going, Anna. *(Anna starts to sing Brahms' "Lullaby," rocking her very gently. Gerald enters)*

GERALD: Hello. I didn't know you did singing lessons as well. Careful, Anna! *(Turns on the lights)*

EILEEN: Get me to bed, Anna, for God's sake.

ANNA: I will go and prepare. *(Exit)*

EILEEN: Take me away from this damn window, Gerald. It's cold. And fetch me a shawl. *(He does so. Trying to be lighthearted, he flourishes the shawl like a toreador)*

GERALD: *Olé!*

EILEEN: You came in at exactly the wrong moment. You usually do. *(He knocks the chair against some furniture)* Clumsy. Oh well, it was probably best, your interrupting. I was in danger of getting sentimental. Wait a minute Gerald, don't mess up what I've asked you to do. . . . Don't tell me when or how. I don't want to know. And make it very certain and sure, so I can't be revived. I don't want stomach pumps, mind you, or a miserable waking up in a hospital bed. I've had enough of that already. I just want to die. You believe in the right to die, it's your credo. You're a coward and a hypocrite if you don't act on it.

GERALD: You're trying to take revenge on God, aren't you?

EILEEN: If God is dead, then sometimes we have to have the courage to act in His place. This is one of those times.

GERALD: *(Phoney laugh)* If you're asking me to play God, I'll have to get a good night's sleep first.

EILEEN: I'm not going to let you get away with your contemptible donnish excuses. Swear you'll do it. Swear on the Bible.

GERALD: Don't be silly. You don't believe in the Bible.

EILEEN: No, but I think you might. Anyway, swear on whatever you believe in most. Keats, Shelley, the BBC. *(Gasping)*

GERALD: I believe you mean it. You really mean it.

(Enter Anna)

ANNA: Your bed is ready, Eileen. *(She starts to wheel her away)*

Blackout

ACT II

Piano music off during scene shift. Morn-
ing a week later. Bright sunlight. The
room is full of flowers, some arranged in
vases, some lying on chairs or tables,
waiting to be attended to. Gerald is alone
on stage trying ineffectively to arrange
the flowers in their vases and place them
appropriately in the room. He is strained
and frustrated and near the end of his
tether. As he moves around the room he
is reciting poetry to himself.

EILEEN: *(Off)* No Anna—it doesn't matter, I tell you.

GERALD: "I looked him round, and looked him through,
Know everything that he will do
In such a case, in such a case,
And when a frown comes on his face
I am afraid, and when a smile
I trace its sources in a while."

(The doorbell rings) Oh, not again!

(Anna entering)

ANNA: It's all right, *Herr* Professor, I'll go. *(Anna goes to the door)*

GERALD: "He cannot do a thing but I
Peep to find the reason why,
For I love him. . . . and I seek

69

Every evening in the week,
To peep behind his frowning eye
With little query, little pry. . . ."

(He knocks a flower vase over and spills it on the floor)

Damn and blast!

(Loud and passionate)

"Yesterday he gripped her tight
And cut her throat—and serve her right."

ANNA: *(Entering)* Is there anything wrong?

GERALD: Nothing, Anna. Just these damned flowers.

ANNA: Let me help you. *(She starts to pick things up)* What must we do with so many flowers?

GERALD: Get rid of them. Send them to a hospital or something. They make the room suffocating. Like a funeral parlour.

ANNA: That's what she says also. But she won't let me take away any one of them. *Herr* Professor, I am worried.

GERALD: You are not the only one.

70

ANNA: She draws more and more into herself.

GERALD: Is she quarrelling and fighting with you, Anna, over every little thing?

ANNA: A little, yes. But that is not the worst. It is worse when she is silent.

GERALD: Reading your thoughts, probing your mind. I'm sorry, Anna. I shouldn't talk like this. You have enough to carry.

ANNA: You also, I think.

GERALD: I just have to say it to someone. I try so hard to control myself, to be patient and understanding at all costs. I feel like an insect on a setting-board with a pin right through me.

EILEEN: Oh, Anna!

ANNA: Coming, Eileen. *(To herself)* I have not a minute to myself. *(Exits. Returns pushing Eileen)*

EILEEN: Ooh—a garden is a lovesome thing, God wot!

ANNA: I go and wash the dishes. *(Exit to kitchen)*

GERALD: *(Trying to restrain himself)* Is there anything I can do for you, dear, before I go down to the College?

EILEEN: I don't think so, thanks.

GERALD: Like me to read some of these letters and cards? They still keep pouring in.

EILEEN: No, don't bother.

GERALD: You must admit at least you've got plenty of fans.

EILEEN: Anna can read them to me. Good for her English.

GERALD: Sure you're quite comfortable?

EILEEN: Quite, thanks. You'd better go to your pupils and tell them about romantic love in the seventeenth century.

GERALD: I don't need to go yet. There's plenty of time.

EILEEN: Do you carry the theme on to the twentieth century? I'd be interested to know what you make of that. Romantic love in the Vickory household! *(Gerald is silent)* Poor, poor Gerald, who so wanted children. I can just see them, clustered on your knee while dear daddy reads them *The Wind in the Willows*, and dear

72

mummy deals with the wind in other less convenient places. Anyway, it's too late for me to bear you a child. Nothing like that for me now. But what about Anna? She would give you a child most willingly.

GERALD: *(Furious)* You're a sad, mad, bitter woman, drowned in your own self-pity. You use your helplessness like a scalpel to cut people open. You sit there in that damned wheelchair like a mummified tyrant sprawling on a throne. Now I understand why you want to die. You hate life, not just in yourself but in everyone else as well. *(Breaking down)* I'm sorry—I'm sorry. I swore I'd never say it, and I have.

EILEEN: You've said what you really think at last. Well, you know the answer, don't you?

GERALD: I refuse to speak about it; I refuse to think about it.

EILEEN: And you know why? Not for love of me, or for any considerations of respect for life. Nothing like that. Just because you're incapable of bringing anything to fulfilment. You talk and you think and you dream, but it's all a nothingness. Look what I've asked you to do. You write about it, and talk about it on TV. But you won't *do* it, and I realise now that

73

you never will and you never can. You're constitutionally impotent. That's why. Impotent.

GERALD: I think I'd better go. *(Exit. We hear the front door slam)*

(Enter Anna. She brings a basin with water and towel)

ANNA: *Herr* Professor has left early.

EILEEN: That's right.

ANNA: I heard him. He clapped the door.

EILEEN: No, Anna. *Herr* Professor—if you must call him that—"slammed" the door. "Slammed" is the word.

ANNA: *Herr* Professor slammed the door. Rather hardly.

EILEEN: No. Not "rather hardly," "Very hard."

ANNA: Very hard. My English! It is terrible this morning. It is always so when I am upset.

EILEEN: So you are upset too.

ANNA: A little. Do I wash and dress you?

EILEEN: I wish you wouldn't use that expression.

What do you think it's like being "washed and dressed"?

ANNA: I put you back then to bed.

EILEEN: Oh, "put me" anywhere you like. I don't care.

ANNA: I leave you then.

EILEEN: No!

ANNA: Perhaps is better.

EILEEN: Don't go. Now that we're here, we may as well stay. I'm sorry, Anna. I got out of bed—no, I was taken out of bed—on the wrong side this morning.

ANNA: I do not understand. It is the same side always, of the bed.

EILEEN: Never mind. Let's change the subject. Read me some of these letters and cards.

ANNA: They are beautiful flowers. The people who send them, it means that they care.

EILEEN: In a ghoulish kind of way.

ANNA: Some of the cards with the flowers are very strange. Rip. R.I.P. What is Rip?

EILEEN: *(Amused)* Rip is a way of saying "Get well soon."

ANNA: Oh. That's nice.

EILEEN: Don't bother, Anna. Most of these people are mad.

ANNA: This one comes from Delia, from Littlehampton-on-Sea. Who is Delia?

EILEEN: What is she? Delia is probably a nut.

ANNA: Her house is called "The Nook." *Ja.* I read from Delia?

EILEEN: You may as well try.

ANNA: "Dear Eileen, Please let me call you Eileen. I would like to take care of you. I have two dogs, six cats, five goldfish and a bud—bud—budger—. . . ." What's a budger?

EILEEN: Hold it here. Let's see. "I have two dogs, six cats, five goldfish and a budgerigar. I feel sure that there is a corner for you, too, in The Nook. I am a true lover of all living creatures. Love, Delia." Oh dear. *(Anna is roaring with laughter. Eileen is amused too. A new warmth is building between them)*

ANNA: *(Laughing)* What is a budger . . . ? I still don't know.

EILEEN: It is a small bird in a cage. Very suitable. They sometimes say . . . very silly things, like me.

ANNA: Well, I hope it says more sense than Delia. *Ja.* This one is from a man, I think.

EILEEN: Oooh. You'd better let me read it. "Dear Eileen, Will you marry me. I could tell at once from your TV programme that that so-called husband of yours is nothing but a half-boiled egg-head, and no earthly good for a red-blooded gal like you. With such a half-dead mate as yours, I don't wonder you feel like dying at times. Why not give me a chance? Believe me, I've been looking for the right partner and you're it. Here's hoping, Ted." Well!

ANNA: This one is from a little boy. "Dear Eileen, I would like to learn to type with my toes. Can you help me? Love, Billy, aged 10."

EILEEN: I wonder if he's as incapacitated as I am. Or is it just for fun? Or to impress his friends?

ANNA: Here is another one. "Dear Eileen, I understand how you feel, but I could never do what you suggest. I am too curious about tomorrow. Please give life another chance. . . . I have been almost totally paralysed for twelve years. . . . I have. . . ."

EILEEN: Show it to me please. "I have a husband and four children. I think and I hope they need me. You see, most wives and mothers are always rushing about all over the place. One thing about me, I'm always there." *(A pause)* Yes, I'm always there. *(We hear the sound of church bells in the distance)* Why are the church bells ringing? It isn't Sunday.

ANNA: It is the day of All Saints.

EILEEN: Ought you to be at mass?

ANNA: I wanted to go. But now *Herr* Professor left so quickly, I must stay with you.

EILEEN: He never understands what other people have in mind.

ANNA: It is equal. I will go later.

EILEEN: Yes, you must do that.

ANNA: All Saints' is a great day in our village. Even the cattle is decorated.

EILEEN: I think you ought to go home, Anna. You belong there.

ANNA: Do you wish that I shall leave you?

EILEEN: No, Anna, I need you—I really do. But I am thinking of someone other than myself for once. I think I often hurt you. I'm afraid I might hurt you more.

ANNA: I think, as long as you need me, I will stay.

EILEEN: Thank you, Anna. *(There are tears in her eyes. Anna wipes away a tear. Front doorbell rings)*

EILEEN: That may be Fergus Whatsisname. He mentioned that he might look in sometime today.

ANNA: I have not any trust this Fergus. I tell him *Herr* Professor is absent.

EILEEN: I'm the one he wants to see. Anyway, we can't leave him on the doorstep. Let him in and put me over there, by the television.

ANNA: Do you want your make-up? Your hair? I have not even washed your face yet.

EILEEN: Don't bother. I'll look pale and tragic. It'll

appeal to his sense of drama. And, Anna, don't be afraid. He won't eat you.

ANNA: I'm not so sure. *(Exits)*

EILEEN: *(To herself)* I'm always here.

(Anna returns ushering in Fergus with large bouquet of flowers)

EILEEN: Come in, Fergus—I'm in here.

FERGUS: *(Seeing all the other flowers)* Oh, dear. Coals to Newcastle. *(Hands bouquet to Anna)*

EILEEN: Come in and sit down. Anna will get you a cup of coffee or something. Or would you like a drink?

FERGUS: No, no, nothing, thank you. I shouldn't be intruding at this unearthly hour, but we happen to be here in Oxford with a crew, filming a minor riot at the annual meeting of the Poetry Society. The crew are setting it up now.

EILEEN: The riot?

FERGUS: It happens every year. We add a little encouragement.

EILEEN: I know. Gerald's usually in the thick of it.

FERGUS: Is he? Is he indeed? It makes first-class television and this year we hope it'll be specially good visually. We did think it would be a good idea, if you're agreeable, to take a few background shots here as well for the programme we discussed. You remember?

EILEEN: You move fast.

FERGUS: When we're on to a good thing we do. Mrs. Vickory—Eileen, if you'll allow me—the response to your programme has been fantastic. What you've got here, the flowers and all, is only a tiny sample. We have had nothing like it on *Way of Life* since the baby-battering last spring.

(Anna expresses her disapproval by shaking the bouquet)

EILEEN: All right, Anna, we needn't keep you. And put those beautiful flowers in some water. There's a dear.

ANNA: As you say. *(Comes over to Eileen)* I must be sure your alarm bell is working properly. Try it, please.

EILEEN: *(Rings alarm bell)* Anna never leaves a thing to chance.

FERGUS: Fantastic. Phenomenal. We must get a

close-up of all that. May I? *(Fergus rings bell with finger)* Just the sort of thing we want. All the little human details.

ANNA: You will ring if you need me.

EILEEN: Thank you, Anna. *(Exit Anna)*

FERGUS: And the girl. Anna, is it?

EILEEN: Mmm.

FERGUS: Ideal. Her watchful care and devotion.

EILEEN: You don't know the half of it.

FERGUS: That strong, Germanic stance and expression. Peasant. Of the earth. Photographically, a marvellous contrast.

EILEEN: But we're jumping ahead. Tell me what you have in mind for the programme.

FERGUS: *Way of Life* has been going well for about ten months. And in that time the audience has been steadily growing, until now we have got one of the highest ratings among the serious programmes.

EILEEN: *(To herself)* Really?

FERGUS: *(Uneasily)* We thought it would interest viewers to take them through your day.

You know—waking up in the morning.

EILEEN: That would be thrilling.

FERGUS: Then being got up—how you manage breakfast, then how you pass the morning, reading the papers, if you do, typing some letters.

EILEEN: Interviewing TV producers.

FERGUS: That typing with your toes—you know, that's the kind of thing that is going to absolutely fascinate the viewers.

EILEEN: Yes. We had a letter today from a little boy of ten, who wants to learn to type with his toes. Fairly representative of your viewers? I tell you what. *(She rings her alarm bell with her toe)* I'll ask Anna to fix up the typewriter for you to see.

(Enter Anna)

ANNA: You are all right?

EILEEN: Yes, I'm all right. But will you please fix up my electronic typewriter for me?

ANNA: You want to type now?

EILEEN: No, but I want to show our guest how we work it. He may want to film us later.

ANNA: *(Does it sulkily)* We must show the world how you type a letter?

FERGUS: Please, I beg you, don't think that this is just pandering to idle curiosity. I assure you, it isn't. That's not *Way of Life*'s style at all. We calculate that watching you overcome your disability, in the truly wonderful way you do, will encourage others who are similarly afflicted, besides creating sympathy.
(He watches Anna as she reluctantly finds and attaches the typewriter with a kind of shoe attached to Eileen's foot)
That is beautifully visual. I would like to do some close-ups of the toes actually at work.

ANNA: That is all?

EILEEN: No. Paper, Anna. I can't type without paper.

FERGUS: *(While Anna is adjusting paper, etc.)* It goes without saying, too, that we'd associate the programme with an appeal for money for medical research. You'd be amazed to know how much we can raise in this way. For instance, the programme we did on the famine in Central Africa— with some really harrowing shots; our commentator just couldn't stop his voice

84

breaking and his eyes filling with tears—
that brought in over a million pounds. I
shouldn't expect as much as that, but I'm
sure we'd do pretty well. A programme
we did on epilepsy, which was very exciting to look at, brought in well over two
hundred thousand. We ought to match
that, if not improve on it.

EILEEN: *(To Anna)* It's not quite straight on my
foot.

ANNA: What speed do you want, Eileen?

EILEEN: Number four. Now, let's see, what shall
we write?

FERGUS: Whatever you think suitable.

EILEEN: *(Typing)* "Way of Life"—produced by
Mr. Fergus Frost.

FERGUS: Snow.

EILEEN: Of course. It must have been a Freudian
slip of the toe. You do realise, Fergus, I
take it, that a programme about my day
won't be quite as pretty and appealing as
you imagine? I can't do anything for myself, and I mean anything. I won't go into
details, but if you want to, you can ask
Anna.

FERGUS: The more adult, the more realistic, the better. We have a very mature public. I shall certainly want to talk to Anna.

EILEEN: Good luck to you. *(Types again)*

ANNA: So now they must all see you taking a bath. *(Exit)*

EILEEN: What do you think of this? Look.

FERGUS: *(Reading what Eileen has typed)* "Way of Life" presents "Way of Death." I don't quite get that.

EILEEN: Don't you?

FERGUS: No.

EILEEN: You are so keen on being adult and mature. The truth, the whole truth, and nothing but the truth. The camera cannot lie. All right, give them the whole truth.

FERGUS: But of course.

EILEEN: Your viewers have heard me say I want to die. Maybe they think I didn't really mean it. Maybe you think that, too. Well then, let's show them that I do mean it.

FERGUS: Mmm.

EILEEN: On behalf of the BBC, after all, a humane, enlightened, and progressive institution if ever there was one, and at my earnest and considered request, you kindly administer to me an appropriate draught for a painless, quick death, just as they did to Socrates. I want to float out, under the camera's eye, so that everyone watching may know that it's possible for a human being, pressed too hard, to decide calmly and resolutely, not buoyed up by an expectation of a life beyond this, to die. How about that for a programme?

FERGUS: Do please go on, I'm not quite with you yet.

EILEEN: Not with me? It's as simple as could be. The cameras roll, and after a short dialogue in which I convince you that I really and truly want to die and die *now*, you obligingly mix the poison, raise the cup to my lips, and with a word of acknowledgment to The Corporation, I swallow the contents, settle into my pillow, and quietly pass out and die. Then the cameras zoom in for a long, lingering close-up; Anna rushes in screaming; my husband is distressed but not shocked and delivers himself of some eloquent sentences to the effect that, though he must mourn the loss of a beloved wife, he takes comfort in the thought that her death will help bring relief to other unwanted lives by advancing the day when all civilised people will accept the right of human beings to die as and when they think fit.

FERGUS: Of course it would be sensational. Fantastic! But could you do it? I mean, surely we would need a really experienced actress to pull a thing like that off convincingly. Could you really simulate a thing like that?

EILEEN: Do you imagine I'm simulating now, and that if I wanted to I could get up and walk about, and eat and drink and make love, like everyone else? I just happen to want to die, and as I'm too incapacitated to kill myself, someone has to help me. Will you help me, in return for a TV programme that'll give you sky-high ratings and make you famous?

FERGUS: *(To himself)* It would be stepping onto entirely new ground. There'd be no going back. Mrs. Vickory—Eileen—I daren't do it even if I wanted to. It's murder, you know, in the eyes of the law. I'd be a murderer; the BBC would fire me; it would be the end. *(Changing tone)* And even if I was prepared to take it on, I'd have to get authorisation at the very highest level—

the Director General, who'd go to the Governors, who'd go to the P.M., who'd go—heaven knows who she'd go to. God, I suppose.

EILEEN: Or the devil.

(Enter Anna)

ANNA: *(Pointedly)* I think you need coffee.

FERGUS: No, not for me, thank you. Look, I've wasted far too much of your time already—I really must go and alert the crew, and if we may, we'll make a start with the other programme we spoke about—your day-to-day life, how you manage—later in the morning, if that would be possible. As for your other suggestion, I promise to think it over, and even discuss it with one or two people.

EILEEN: In life, in death, oh Lord, trust the BBC.

FERGUS: *(Not sure whether to take it seriously)* Very good. Very good indeed. May we come back later then for those establishing shots?

EILEEN: When you like. I'm always here.

FERGUS: I'll alert the crew then. *Au revoir.* *(To Anna)* Please don't bother to see me out. I can find my own way. *(Exit)*

89

ANNA: *(Angry)* So, he comes back again?

EILEEN: With a crew. He'd like you on the programme.

ANNA: Why?

EILEEN: He wants to show you doing things for me.

ANNA: What things?

EILEEN: Oh, everything. Brushing my hair. Washing my face. Cleaning my teeth.

ANNA: Do I need Mr. Fergus and a camera to brush the hair? To wash the face is to wash the face. Must the whole world see?

EILEEN: You are rather a relief after Fergus. He's a phoney.

ANNA: Phoney? Phoney? I like that word. "You are a phoney. I am a phoney." *(Fetches bowl from nearby)*

EILEEN: No, Anna. You're not a phoney.

ANNA: What does it mean, *phoney*?

EILEEN: It means, not natural, not real, but ersatz.

ANNA: Oh. *(Washes Eileen's face)*

EILEEN: Ow! That water's cold. Get some fresh.

ANNA: Cold water is good. Not phoney.

EILEEN: Yes, but it stings. Keep it out of my eyes, for God's sake.

ANNA: Sorry. *(Anna dries vigorously)*

EILEEN: That towel is rough. You're a bully, Anna.

ANNA: What is bully?

EILEEN: Someone who is deliberately cruel and unkind.

ANNA: Then I am not the only one who is bully. *(Brushes hair)*

EILEEN: Be careful, Anna. You're pulling.

ANNA: It needs much brush. *Herr* Professor, he comes soon from the university. He likes to see *Frau* Professor looking pretty.

EILEEN: Don't be silly. You should have heard him this morning.

ANNA: I did. That is because he tries to love and does not know how.

EILEEN: That's certainly true!

ANNA: And you? You know how?

EILEEN: Yes, but I'm useless.

ANNA: No one is useless. Nothing is useless, if it helps someone to love.

EILEEN: That's a very pretty theory. But why me? Why me?

ANNA: Why not you? Now let me look at those finger claws.

EILEEN: Nails! Or are they claws?

ANNA: I think you make *Herr* Professor feeling sometimes, that he is less than a man. Could you not love him into being a man? *Herr* Professor tries to love you, I think.

EILEEN: How can I love him? I can't even fling my arms around his neck. I can't hug him and kiss him. I can't even stretch out a hand to take his.

ANNA: Is love just to fling the arms, to hug and kiss?

EILEEN: Most people think that's quite important.

ANNA: Of course. But not all. Sister Magdalena gives me once a picture.

EILEEN: Who is Sister Magdalena?

ANNA: One of the nuns at school. She was very old. Not for her to fling the arms, to hug and kiss. And yet, in her face, much love. The picture she gave me, I have it still in my Bible. Look, here it is. *(She takes picture from Bible and shows it to Eileen)* The man on the cross, more helpless than you. He cannot move arms or legs, and He is dying. Sister Magdalena said He has filled the world with love, not just then, but forever.

EILEEN: I know about Him too, and it doesn't help me.

ANNA: But Eileen, you do not try.

EILEEN: I'm sure your nuns are very worthy people, but poverty, chastity, and obedience are not my choice. I've had a cloistered life thrust on me.

ANNA: There was another Sister in the convent, Sister Paula. She becomes very ill, so she shakes all over like this. We girls are very unkind. We laugh behind her back and, how you say . . . *(Mimics)*

EILEEN: Mimic.

ANNA: That's right. Mimic. Sister Magdalena

saw us. She was angry. "If Sister Paula shakes, she shakes for the glory of God," she said. "Sister Paula helps me to live with foolish, naughty girls like you. By her prayers she is my *Kraftwerk.*" You know, where electric is made. "My *Kraftwerk* of love."

EILEEN: "Powerhouse" we call it. I'm afraid it's the other way round with me. I'm no generator of love; only rather a heavy consumer.

(There is a sound at the front door)

ANNA: There is *Herr* Professor.

EILEEN: *(Listens anxiously)* He's not even coming in to say hello, as he always does. He must be feeling angry.

ANNA: He goes to the kitchen.

EILEEN: Look, Anna, you must help me. You are right. I am a bully. I always have been. It's too long since I've loved Gerald properly. Even so, go and get him, Anna. Ask him if he'll come in and see me.

ANNA: Not phoney?

EILEEN: Not phoney.

ANNA: Then I think you will have good luck.

EILEEN: Wait a minute. Give me one of those flowers, Anna. One of the roses. No, not that. The red one behind. Put it by me. Put it in my hand. Now go and get Gerald. And Anna, leave us alone. Go and practise. Or do you want to go to mass?

ANNA: Later. It is at midday. I go later. *(Exit)*

(After a pause Gerald enters with cup of coffee)

EILEEN: Gerald. That's very thoughtful. Just what I was wanting. Will you fix it for me?

EILEEN: Perfect. *(We hear Anna begin to play)* How did the lecture go?

GERALD: It was cancelled. Not enough there.

EILEEN: It's such a beautiful day.

GERALD: Yes, isn't it.

EILEEN: All your students were probably out enjoying themselves.

GERALD: Probably.

EILEEN: What was the lecture going to be on?

GERALD: Blake. Blake's imagery.

EILEEN: Say some to me; say some Blake.

GERALD: Not now.

EILEEN: Please.

GERALD: I give you the end of a golden string,
          Only wind it into a ball;
          It will lead you in at Heaven's gate,
          Built in Jerusalem's wall.

EILEEN: That's lovely.

GERALD: Is the coffee all right?

EILEEN: Very good. Nice and strong.

GERALD: Well, I'll leave you to it, if you don't mind.

EILEEN: *(Drinks)* Gerald, please come to me.

          (He comes to her. She looks at the flower)

GERALD: *(Picking up flower)* Do you want this thing? Shall I take it away?

EILEEN: *(Pause as she drinks)* It's for you.

GERALD: For me? Why?

EILEEN: I thought you might like it. Take it, Gerald. It won't bite you. I wish I could pin it on for you.

GERALD: Oh, for God's sake, shall I tell Anna to stop playing?

EILEEN: No, Gerald. I just wanted to say that I'm sorry.

GERALD: Sorry?

EILEEN: Yes, for the unpleasantness, the bad temper.

GERALD: Oh please, not now. Don't think of it.

EILEEN: I suppose it's all part of the intolerable pressure we've all lived under. I'm certain I'll get it all wrong, but do you think we could possibly . . .

(Her voice fades)

GERALD: *(Agonised voice)* Have you finished the coffee?

EILEEN: Yes, it was good. . . . *(Realisation)* Gerald, your timing's not very good is it? What a mess we've made of it all. Those first days so innocent, especially you. The real illness was in me always. *(Panic)*

Gerald, I can't see you. Stay with me. Hold my hand. I'm getting sleepy. There's something I must do for you, so that they know I shamed you into it . . . the coffee . . .

(With an enormous effort, Eileen begins to type, speaking the words as she spells them out)
He . . . did . . . it . . . for . . . me. *(Gasp)* I . . . made . . . him. I . . . I . . . *(Dies)*

(Anna enters, looks, and goes to Eileen's side—moves her head)

(Gerald puts down Eileen's hand, goes to telephone, dials 999. Fergus with two cameramen enters and watches from doorway)

GERALD: Police? This is Gerald Vickory, 24 Garsington Road, Oxford. I want to report a death. My wife. This is her husband. I'm responsible. She's dead.

(Anna sobs)

FERGUS: *(Indicating to cameramen)* Get it!

(Lights focus very strongly on body in chair)

Blackout

END OF ACT II

ACT III

ACT III

Spring, four months later. The room is exactly as before, but without the flowers. The empty wheelchair is in its place. Outside we can hear sounds of the press. Subdued babble of voices.

ANNA: *(Shouting)* Go away! Leave me alone, I say! *Weg, weg! (Door banged and locked. Enter Anna with doctor)*

DR. WINTER: I'm sorry if I scared you. I had to get in somehow.

ANNA: Of course. I thought it was the big man again who made to come in before. He had a camera. I am lucky I know how to push a fat bull out of the barn.

DR. WINTER: It's just a circus out there.

ANNA: But what is the news, *Herr* Doctor? He comes?

DR. WINTER: There was no news at one. The jury is still out. All the rest are taking lunch. The judge is having lunch in his chambers. I hope it's a good one.

ANNA: And *Herr* Professor waits.

DR. WINTER: There might be something at two. Oh God—how everybody loves a murder

103

trial. There may be wars, massacres, earthquakes, revolutions all over the world. But what happens to one poor woman, one wretched man, that's the real stuff. *(Phone rings)*

ANNA: Perhaps this tells something. *(Answering phone)* Hello. Yes. Oh, you are it again. I tell you I do not know. No. Please do not ring any more. I can tell you nothing. I am only the maid. No I can't. *"I' sog's Ihnen, i' weiss nichts. I' bin nur's Mädchen. Bitte, gehn's weg und lassen's mich in Ruh' O, gehn's zum Teifel."* *(Slams down receiver)* That stops him!

DR. WINTER: You're learning.

ANNA: Another who comes to the door says he wants the "low-down." "You are the low-down," I say. It is good that you are here, doctor. Can I get you something—cognac?

DR. WINTER: That's not a bad idea. Thanks. I really couldn't stand that court another minute. Those brutal faces. All those sensation-mongers. The usual trendy clergyman looking for next Sunday's sermon topic.

Thank you. Aren't you having one?

ANNA: No.

DR. WINTER: Cheers.

The "Right to Die" fanatics, buzzing with zeal and their latest propaganda. Lady Bassett of course, much in evidence, whispering to Counsel and the solicitors, organising everything. I suppose she cares.

ANNA: But will he come?

DR. WINTER: The press out there evidently expect him. They usually sniff out these things. Heaven knows it will be a great triumph if he gets off; and you know I've a hunch that, thanks to Eileen's last message, he will get off; well, he'll be pretty exhausted. But I am grateful you are here, Anna. You have made everything look fine, just as it was. The chair? Is that really wise?

ANNA: I change nothing. It is hers and *Herr* Professor's. I try her piano. But I could not play.

DR. WINTER: I am sure it is not easy for you to come back here. I understand you found lodgings and another job.

ANNA: *Ja.*

DR. WINTER: He provided for you, I hope.

ANNA: For the house, of course. For me, I would take nothing. I worked in the hospital as a cleaning woman. Not very nice work, but I would rather that than be here. There they try to cure people. I have never entered this house. A house of death, of murder.

DR. WINTER: He did what he did out of love, Anna. You must believe that.

ANNA: I do not think he knows what love is.

DR. WINTER: Oh?

ANNA: When that man at the court, him with the false grey hair, said to me again and again, "Do you love him? Did you love him?" . . . what am I to say? Sometimes I want to cry out to all the people, "I do not love him. I hate him. I saw what he did." And then, as I see him there, in the box with the policeman, then I almost feel, "I do not hate him, I love him." Because he suffers.

DR. WINTER: I'm glad you did not say that in court. The Prosecuting Counsel was trying to make out it was a dirty little sex crime. That Gerald killed her, because he wanted you for himself.

ANNA: That man who says that is a monster. He is mad.

DR. WINTER:	No. He's just doing his job. He's probably a very nice chap really. Loves his wife and children.
ANNA:	He has wife and children? I pity them.
DR. WINTER:	You have never been in a law court before. Anyway, you did well, Anna. You stood up to him splendidly. I think your evidence will have helped a lot.
ANNA:	I hope so.
DR. WINTER:	Well, as far as you're concerned, it's all over now, isn't it?
ANNA:	But it goes round and round inside. It must come out.
DR. WINTER:	Of course. You have had a hard time. It's brave of you to stay. You could have gone straight back to Germany after giving your evidence.
ANNA:	*Ja.* I know. But there is one task before. I must end correctly my employment. I must give my accounts. If he comes . . . he will need food. I prepare his room. I fetch the newspapers of today. The *Times* and the *Guardian.* He reads always the *Times* and the *Guardian.* I find, what you say, his crossword puzzle and so on. Then if I want, I can go home.

DR. WINTER: You've really become part of the family, haven't you? The great thing, as you say, Anna, is to try and treat everything normally if he does come back home. Everything is ready for him to resume his old life. He's an intelligent and balanced man. What he did, he did deliberately, with his eyes open, according to his principles and hers, poor soul; and when all's said and done, he acted perfectly rationally. It was what she most deeply wanted.

ANNA: Oh, doctor, you were not here. It was not like that. I saw her as she died. I saw him holding her hand, with the coffee cup beside her. I saw him go to the phone. Those terrible men with their cameras. Was that, as you say, rational?

(Gerald is standing in the room. He has on an overcoat and scarf. He is pale, at times shaky, but unexpected and strange)

DR. WINTER: Gerald! My dear fellow. *(Gerald staggers a little)* Come and sit down. You're free?

GERALD: *(Laughs)* Free.

ANNA: I get you something. Some wine, food.

GERALD: No, thank you. Nothing. They feed you at the court. Fatten you up. Like a pig before the carve-up—all shiny with an apple in your mouth. I'd like a glass of water, please.

ANNA: *Ja,* of course. *(Exit)*

GERALD: I was declared guilty. Two years' imprisonment. Suspended.

DR. WINTER: Thank God.

GERALD: In the old days they suspended the criminal. "To be hanged by the neck until you are dead. And may the Lord have mercy on your soul." Now they suspend the sentence instead of the criminal. Strange. Comic, really. *(Enter Anna with water)* Thank you. It's good that you are both here.

DR. WINTER: How did you get here?

GERALD: A police car.

DR. WINTER: All the press outside.

GERALD: We came in by the back door. One of the policemen said, "You're famous, you know, now." A quite good English literature don, an author of one or two learned books. And who cares? A murderer—famous. I think I'll have more water, if you don't mind.

109

ANNA: Only water.

GERALD: Thank you. I feel terribly thirsty.

DR. WINTER: That's all right, Gerald. Rest. Relax. You're safe now. And, my dear fellow, I can't tell you how glad we are you're free.

GERALD: Guilty. The last part in court, with the verdict and sentence, is crystal clear. Other things are a jumble. Confused, like one of those nightmares when you are always trying to get somewhere and you never do. Oh, believe me, I seem to be mad at times, utterly mad. "Guilty." *(Laughs)* The judge was so exactly like me, talking to a pupil who'd failed to come up with his weekly essay: "I am, in this case, taking into account the jury's recommendation of mercy. Also the words of your dying wife, typed as death was overtaking her. 'He did it for me. I made him.' " *(He suddenly breaks down)*

DR. WINTER: That's all right, Gerald. Don't try to talk.

GERALD: I have to talk, to explain. It's such a relief to have someone to talk to.

(A ring at the door)

DR. WINTER: Don't bother.

GERALD: Then after the verdict, it's all jumble again. Shouting. People singing "We shall overcome," trampling all over one another to reach me, touch me. Connie Bassett to the fore. She threatened to come here. *(Bell rings again)* It might be her.

DR. WINTER: I'll go and see. *(Exit)*

ANNA: I had better leave you.

GERALD: No. Stay, Anna. Stay. *(Voices at the door)* It is Connie. She's a wonderful person really. I must do my best.

(Dr. Winter leads in Lady Bassett. She is smartly turned out, tall, bony, with considerable charm and forcefulness. Loud voice and over-cultured accent)

LADY BASSETT: My dear, Gerald. No, no, no. Please don't get up. You must be utterly exhausted.
(But he does so)

GERALD: Connie. It is good of you to come.

LADY BASSETT: *(Taking both his hands)* Gerald! I just felt I had to squeeze my way in. I won't stay more than a minute.

GERALD: I saw you in court.

LADY BASSETT: I had to come, Anna. Just as a friend. To shake you by the hand. I know this isn't the time or the place. *(She puts her bag down on the wheelchair)* But I couldn't let this great day go by without . . .

GERALD: *(Hypnotised by the wheelchair)* Please take it away, Connie.

LADY BASSETT: What's the matter?

GERALD: *(Shouts)* Take it away!

ANNA: Please, let me. *(She removes bag)*

LADY BASSETT: How thoughtless of me, Gerald. Forgive me. Now, Gerald, I'm not going to stay. I just have to say this. Quite simply. We have always admired you and valued your support, perhaps—if you understand me—as a thinker, a theoretician for the cause, more than—what shall I say?—an activist.

GERALD: *(Vaguely)* Thank you, Connie. Very kind.

LADY BASSETT: How wrong we were! How utterly, utterly wrong! You, and your beloved wife, whom we shall always honour equally, you have made the great breakthrough.

GERALD: *(A cry)* What?

DR. WINTER: You realise, of course, how exhausted he is.

LADY BASSETT: Oh, of course, I realise so fully. That's why I'm here. To tell you that we all understand. Take your time. But never lose hold of this. This is a great day, not just for you personally. You are vindicated before the whole world. But it is also a great day for British justice.

GERALD: Guilty!

LADY BASSETT: You are only technically guilty, Gerald. My bill in the Lords, which, as I think you know, is reaching its critical stage in Parliament, is aimed to alter all that. With the proper legislation, you would have been spared this frightful ordeal.

GERALD: Connie, I must try to explain. . . . I wouldn't have been spared for all the world.

LADY BASSETT: Gerald, take my advice. Don't try to explain anything now. You are overwrought.

GERALD: *(Angry)* I am not overwrought. I am try-

ing to explain something vital . . . rele-
vant . . . the whole point, really . . .

DR. WINTER: I really don't think this is the time or
place.

LADY
BASSETT: No, no, of course. But you can take
strength from the fact that you have done
far, far more than you can possibly realise. Why, all the truly great social re-
forms have come about through the posi-
tive action of one man or one woman.
The suffrage movement, the new abortion laws. Always one great fighter, one
reformer has led the way.

DR. WINTER: I really must insist—

LADY
BASSETT: In fact, in full anticipation of your freedom, I have arranged a little informal
gathering in the Connaught Rooms next
Monday night. Nothing alarming, I assure you. A few drinks and speeches.
Some toasts. And then, one or two words
from you—if you're up to it, of course.
Strike while the iron is hot!

GERALD: Connie, this iron is not hot.

LADY
BASSETT: You see, my bill, as I say, is at a very cru-
cial stage and your action has been so
timely.

GERALD: *(In growing anger)* Excuse me, Connie, do I understand that you want to use me, and Eileen, as propaganda for your bill?

LADY BASSETT: Oh no, no, not use, I assure you. But you will naturally want to help. . . . Where was I?

GERALD: I don't know where you are. I wish I could explain to you where I am. I wish I could explain to myself.

LADY BASSETT: Gerald, you and your beloved Eileen have set the great example. But now let us carry the torch that you have so magnificently lit. I'm just a servant, a very humble servant in the ultimate of all human rights, the right to die.

GERALD: *(With enormous restraint, trying to sound sane)* Yes, the right to die. Listen to me, Connie. Have you ever thought of claiming that right for yourself. . . ?

LADY BASSETT: I'm sorry, Gerald. I don't quite understand.

GERALD: Would it not enormously further the cause you hold so dear, if *you* were to exercise your right . . . and volunteer . . . to. . . . Forgive me. I don't know what I'm saying . . .

DR. WINTER:	You can see that he needs absolute rest and quiet.
LADY BASSETT:	Yes, of course. He has suffered even more than I realised. Another time, Gerald. But we will meet soon.
DR. WINTER:	Goodbye. Thank you so much for coming. Let me show you out.
LADY BASSETT:	Time is a great healer, Gerald. Until the Connaught Rooms. *(She and doctor go out)*
GERALD:	I'd die for the right never to have to listen to that woman again. *(Doctor re-enters)* She's not going to turn me into a humanist saint!
DR. WINTER:	O.K., Gerald, take it easy.
GERALD:	Of course, there are advantages to being slightly mad. You can say what you like.
DR. WINTER:	You'll soon be yourself again.
GERALD:	Do you know, of all the terrors, that's the greatest terror of all, that I will be myself again. That I'll wake up tomorrow morning and be my old self again. I'm sorry. I know you meant it kindly. Thank you, Derek. Your evidence helped me a lot. And you, Anna.

ANNA: Let me get you something. I will cook for you specially your favourite.

GERALD: When I was in there I often longed for your cooking. Now I couldn't swallow a thing.

ANNA: I know one thing. *Glühwein.* I get it. *(Exit)*

DR. WINTER: My poor fellow, you're looking absolutely all in, and no wonder after what you've been through.

GERALD: Prison in itself wasn't so bad. I'm glad I insisted on refusing bail. In fact, I almost liked prison in a way. At times it seemed strangely familiar—not unlike Senior Common Room, really. Not so comfortable, of course. But the company—each one's an expert in his way, a specialist who knows more and more about less and less. The ones in for sex offences and fraud, they were like economists and natural science dons, very opinionated; my lot, in for crimes of violence, were a bit fanatical and pedantic, given to splitting hairs, like theologians; then the con-men and burglars, they were almost as long-winded as sociologists. And of course you meet the odd and occasional saint, just as surprising and disconcerting there as anywhere else. Sorry, I'm wandering.

The pressure cooker heats to a certain point and then the lid blows off. I am glad you're here.

DR. WINTER: I only wish I could have helped more.

GERALD: I thought of coming to you when she asked me to do it. "Excuse me, doctor, I'm thinking of killing my wife. Give me a few useful tips, will you?" You'd have thought me mad. Still do, I daresay.

DR. WINTER: No, Gerald. All the same, I wish you had come to see me. I've thought of that often. I suppose I could have helped. You see, she asked me to do what . . . you did. I suppose I could have got away with it. Doctors can. I could have fulfilled her deepest wish and spared you . . . all this.

GERALD: Why didn't you?

DR. WINTER: Well, to start with, I couldn't believe she really meant it.

GERALD: Nor could I.

DR. WINTER: I took it as a sort of passing phase. Up one minute, down the next. You know how women are.

GERALD: Do I?

DR. WINTER: In any case, I just wouldn't consider it. Cowardice, I suppose. Not moral considerations—in the ordinary sense. Not much to do with right and wrong. Morals for me are just doing the best I can for all concerned. No, what weighed with me, I think, was a more practical consideration. After all the effort we'd made to keep her alive, it seemed rather like going to endless pains to shore up some collapsing building, and then calling in the demolition men on the grounds that the building was useless and empty.

GERALD: You'd have got away with it, you say?

DR. WINTER: Doctors nowadays get away with a good deal.

GERALD: You wouldn't. Oh, for a time, I thought I would. At first I felt like a kind of a hero, a martyr for a cause. I'd done what she'd begged me to do. I was what that terrible woman called a "pioneer." The first to climb Everest, to cross Niagara Falls on a tight-rope, pushing my wife in a wheelbarrow. Pity I dropped her out on the way, but that was what she wanted, all part of the act. Then the voices began. Principle. The right to die. Death with dignity. And then you're all alone in a prison cell, eight feet by six. Another voice, quite different . . . "Thou shalt do no murder." The prison chaplain got me a Bible. I had to ask for it, mind. Otherwise, he assumed I preferred the latest detective story or the *Times Literary Supplement*. "Thou shalt not kill"—you know, there is almost a kind of peace in calling a thing by its real name.

DR. WINTER: Gerald, I wish I could help more. My instinct is to tell you to take a long rest, go away into the country—abroad, better still. Go for long walks, read Jane Austen: you know what I mean. At any rate, I'll give you a prescription—something to get you to sleep at night and calm you down by day.

GERALD: *(Outburst)* For God's sake, you doctors! I'm sorry, Derek, I know you're trying to help, doing your stuff. But all you've got to offer to someone in desperation, with a sense of guilt like a millstone round his neck is—a prescription! Have you a prescription for millstones? In your eyes we're just bodies. Sick and well—normal and abnormal—sane and crazy; such categories stand for you. But Evil and Good—inadmissible. I am a murderer; just as truly as Jack the Ripper or Crippen, though a very clumsy and foolish one. Even so, I have to tell you that I'm glad—yes, glad—that I didn't avail my-

self of the murder-without-tears the medical profession provides nowadays. Because I've caught a glimpse—not more
than that—of an escape route other than
on the wings of one of your prescriptions,
from the tiny dark dungeon of the ego in
which I've been incarcerated.

DR. WINTER: *(Writing prescription)* All the same I am
going to give you a prescription. And
(producing a bottle) here's something
meanwhile to help you to sleep. Just take
one or two at night. Goodness, look at
the time. I really must be pushing off, got
a hysterectomy and a prostate. Don't forget, call me any time. Bye-bye. Goodbye,
Anna. *(Anna enters with two glasses. She
is dressed for the road—a touch of the Ba-
varian costume)*

ANNA: Oh, goodbye. Oh, I've brought a glass
for the doctor.

GERALD: You drink it, Anna. Cheers.

ANNA: Cheers.

GERALD: How ridiculous! What are we cheering?

ANNA: *Herr* Professor is back.

GERALD: Yes. *(Drinking)* That feels better. You've
kept everything beautifully. Just the

121

same. *(Haunted by chair)* Yes. You had enough money, I hope.

ANNA: Oh yes. We have had people to clean the house, arrange the garden. And I . . . I am not afraid of work. Your bed is made. There is food in the fridge. You will find someone practical.

GERALD: You're not leaving?

ANNA: You will be all right now.

GERALD: We can't just part like this, after everything that's happened.

ANNA: What does *Herr* Professor want to say?

GERALD: I suppose you are the one I have hurt the most . . . that awful time for you in court.

ANNA: *(Indicates: "Don't mention it")*

GERALD: One can't merely say "I'm sorry." It goes too deep. Murder, treachery, hatred, cruelty—those are terrible things, but they're not the worst. They are like a white spot on a man's skin that tells you he's a leper—full of poison. Has there ever been a single moment in my life when I've really faced the truth? All a fantasy.

ANNA: What does a man do when he feels such as that?

GERALD: Quite simple. Either he is finished, damned . . . *(He fingers the pills the doctor gave him)*

ANNA: Or else?

GERALD: Or else he finds a light, a pinprick of hope and sanity.

ANNA: What was that light for you, *Herr* Professor?

GERALD: You.

ANNA: Me?

GERALD: I suppose one could call it purity. Thinking that way in prison brought me, just sometimes, a sort of clarification, an awareness that at the very heart of all existence there lies some absorbing, heartrending, unutterably beautiful, and yet at the same time hilarious mystery, which, once glimpsed, makes everything else an irrelevance, a diversion. Do you understand?

ANNA: The words I do not understand. The man behind the words I think I understand a little.

GERALD: A line of George Herbert kept coming into my mind: "Let me not love thee, if I love thee not." I'd never understood that.

ANNA: To whom speaks this poet? To his mistress?

GERALD: No. To his Lord.

ANNA: Then I understand. Whoever loves Him must love with all his heart or not at all. But cannot the Professor speak for himself?

GERALD: I can't. I need that strength and purity of yours. . . . Anna, could you . . . would you . . . ? Could it be that we could explore that mystery together?

ANNA: *(In wonder)* Oh, *Herr* Professor. You mean it? You? Not poetry?

GERALD: *(With false confidence)* I mean it.

ANNA: No! *(Pauses)* No, no, no, no! It could not ever be. I could never forget . . . what has happened. You remember how I looked after her: things that might have seemed—ugly become so loving and beautiful. And now she's walking about like everyone else. So, you see, I could not. It'll make her laugh, *Herr* Professor, because she thought I was *herzlich* for you. I can hear her laughing. My things are here. *(Anna picks up her rucksack)*

GERALD: Anna!

ANNA: Yes?

GERALD: You are really and truly leaving?

ANNA: Yes.

GERALD: Now?

ANNA: You can do without me. It is best.

GERALD: Are you sure, Anna? Can I really face it all on my own?—the disapproval, the sympathy? Worst of all myself. No wonder I often wish I could die. *(Plays unconsciously with pills)*

ANNA: That is not your punishment, to die.

GERALD: I know. *(Lays pills down)* Sentenced to life. No remission, no parole. Perhaps I will go to the Connaught Rooms after all. Give them a piece of my mind.

ANNA: You mean, not phoney.

GERALD: I will try, Anna, to be not phoney. Tell me, do you have everything?

ANNA: I have what I need. If I have left back something, one day I can return and fetch it.

GERALD: You *have* left something. Thank you, Anna.

ANNA: You remember what she wrote as she died?

GERALD: "He did it for me. I made him."

ANNA: More. There is more.

GERALD: Nothing more. "I . . . I . . ."

ANNA: Oh, *Herr* Professor, you are so clever and yet so foolish. She wanted to say "I love you." She told me it before you came to her that day.

GERALD: Thank you, Anna. *(She kisses him on both cheeks. He helps her on with her pack. She hands him picture from Missal. Exits)*

(For a while Gerald stands there, lost. His eyes are riveted on Eileen's chair. Meanwhile, Fergus and his camera crew appear at the back and in dumb-show set up their lights and cameras ready to film. Fergus is watching and listening intently for the moment when he can shout "Action!"

and begin to film. Gerald is unaware of their presence and they must not distract attention from his speech. Slowly Gerald goes to chair and starts to wheel it a little.)

GERALD: Gently. Gently. *(He knocks the chair)* Oh my dear, that's me. Clumsy still. How were you going to finish that last brave message? *(In anguish)* "I . . . I . . . ." Was it "I love you"? "I . . . love you." So I killed someone who loved me. First getting the poison from the university lab: those little white granules, so harmless-looking, so innocent, then slipping them into the coffee I had made for you—not spilling it, for once; then feeding you the coffee. You drank it so gratefully, so lovingly, like a blood-transfusion. Only it was a death-transfusion, and I watched you suck it down. *(Breaks down)* It was my pride that made me do it, I see it now. You called me . . . impotent. I had to show you. . . . I had to show myself . . . and yet you were right. I could even then have phoned for the doctor in time. But I didn't. I phoned the police instead and told them quietly and deliberately, almost smugly, that I let you die because it was what you said you wanted. A passionless crime; no diminished responsibility or anything like that. No "other woman" for whom I wanted to be free from the encumbrance of a stricken wife. Strangely enough, it would have been less heinous if I'd had a reason like that. It was just a cold-hearted, calculated murder—meting out death for a principle, out of pride. *Oh, my darling, I helped you to die, but I never helped you to live.* That's my real crime. Can a convicted murderer, like the thief on Golgotha, at Christ's side . . . make a fresh start? "This day thou shalt be with me in paradise." "This day thou shalt be with me"—wherever and whoever I may be.

If only you were here now, how different it would be! In our affliction—for yours would be mine and mine yours—we'd find new sources of strength and love, which would bind us together as we never were before. We'd understand, too, the Man on the cross between the thieves. We'd come to see affliction—yours and mine—as part of God's love, enriching, not depriving; creative, not destructive; a fulfilment, not a frustration. If only you were here to help me. If only you were here to help!

(We hear the piano played very softly and beautifully—Beethoven)

It sounds like Anna—no, of course, it's Eileen, Eileen! *(He kneels)*

128

FERGUS: *(Having lost patience at last)* Cut!! It's no good. He's bonkers!

GERALD: *(Still kneeling)* No, sane at last.

(Music rises triumphantly)

THE END